W9-AQT-528

OCT 1970
RECEIVED
OHIO DOMINICAN
COLLEGE LIBRARY
COLUMBUS, OHIO

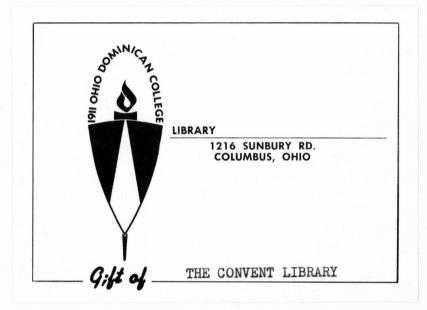

1911 OHIO DOMINICAN COLLEGE

LIBRARY
1216 SUNBURY RD.
COLUMBUS, OHIO

*Gift of* _____ THE CONVENT LIBRARY

Americans All biographies are inspiring life stories about people of all races, creeds, and nationalities who have uniquely contributed to the American way of life. Highlights from each person's story develop his contributions in his special field — whether they be in the arts, industry, human rights, education, science and medicine, or sports.

Specific abilities, character, and accomplishments are emphasized. Often despite great odds, these famous people have attained success in their fields through the good use of ability, determination, and hard work. These fast-moving stories of real people will show the way to better understanding of the ingredients necessary for personal success.

# Robert F. Kennedy

## MAN WHO DARED TO DREAM

by Charles P. Graves

illustrated by Victor Mays

*GARRARD PUBLISHING COMPANY*
*CHAMPAIGN, ILLINOIS*

# For Amy and Tony Beach

**Picture credits:**

Yale Joel, LIFE Magazine © Time Inc.: p. 34

London *Daily Express*—Pictorial Parade: p. 93

*Paris Match*—Pictorial Parade: p. 2, 89 (bottom), 96

Pictorial Parade: p. 22 (top), 82

Arthur Rickerby, LIFE Magazine © Time Inc.: p. 54

Steve Schapiro from Black Star: p. 60 (both)

United Press International: p. 10, 19, 22 (bottom), 51, 64, 89 (top)

J
923.2
K

Copyright © 1970 by Charles P. Graves
All rights reserved. Manufactured in the U.S.A.
Standard Book Number: 8116-4557-6
Library of Congress Catalog Card Number: 76-101302

# Contents

72054

# 1. "Win! Win! Win!"

"Watch me swim!" four-year-old Bobby Kennedy shouted, jumping out of the rowboat into water that was way over his head. He came up coughing and sputtering and flailing the water with both arms.

His twelve-year-old brother, Jack, got ready to dive in and rescue him, but Bobby managed to fight his way back to the boat. Jack pulled him aboard.

"That's my brother," Jack said with a smile. "All guts and no brains. You might have drowned."

"I swam, didn't I?" Bobby bragged, wiping the water from his freckled face. "And I'm going to swim better every day."

Bobby and Jack were rowing on the choppy Cape Cod waters close to their family's summer home at Hyannis Port, Massachusetts. A little farther out to sea, the oldest Kennedy brother, Joe, Jr., aged fourteen, was competing in a sailing race. Bobby and Jack cheered loudly when they saw Joe's boat sweep across the finish line in first place.

The boys' father, Joseph P. Kennedy, Sr., wanted all of his children to be good athletes, and he encouraged them to enter sailing races, swimming meets, and tennis matches. He congratulated them when they won and scolded them when they lost. Victory was almost as necessary as food and drink to the Kennedys.

"Coming in second is no good," Mr. Kennedy told his children. "The important thing is to win! Don't come in second or third—that doesn't count—but win, win, WIN!"

With that kind of advice from his father it is no wonder that, as Bobby grew older, he took part in every kind of sport as if winning were a matter of life or death. He was small for his age, and because he was the seventh of nine children, it wasn't often that he won in family competitions, but he always did his best.

"I had to keep getting better in every way just to survive," he once said.

Robert Francis Kennedy was born in Brookline, Massachusetts, on November 20, 1925. Soon after his birth the Kennedy family moved to New York City and then to Bronxville, a nearby suburb. When he was old enough, Bobby attended public schools. He was shy and didn't make many friends at first, but he always had

When the Kennedys posed for this picture in Bronxville, Bobby (top right) was nine.

someone to play with at home. Besides his two older brothers, he had four older sisters, a younger sister, and a baby brother, Edward, whom everyone called Teddy.

Bobby had pets to play with, too, including a pig named Porky and rabbits that he raised in his back yard and sold to neighbors. Even though Mr. Kennedy was extremely wealthy he wanted his children to earn their own spending money so that they would understand the value of work and money.

The Kennedys employed many servants. Their chauffeur's son was one of Bobby's friends. The two boys often played together, and they both enjoyed planning and carrying out daring adventures.

Once Bobby and his playmate made two parachutes out of some old sheets. Then, carrying their parachutes with them, the boys climbed onto the roof of the Kennedy house and crept to the edge. Looking down, the two "paratroopers" shuddered, and Bobby's face turned white beneath his mop of chestnut hair.

"I-I-I'll jump first," he stammered.

"No! I want to be first," his playmate insisted.

"O.K., go ahead," Bobby said.

Holding his parachute above his head, the boy leaped off the roof and hurtled toward the ground while Bobby watched. To his horror, the parachute did not open.

The boy crashed to the ground with a thud and began screaming with pain. Mrs. Kennedy rushed from the house and tried to comfort the boy. After ordering Bobby to come down from the roof at

once, she hurried into the house and called a doctor.

When the doctor had examined the boy he said, "He'll be all right. It's only a broken leg!"

"Only a broken leg!" Bobby exclaimed enviously. Then he said to himself, "A broken leg is a small price to pay for all the attention he's getting. Next time I'm going to jump first."

## 2. U.S.S. *Joseph P. Kennedy, Jr.*

"It's easy, Bobby," Joe, Jr. said, "just shake hands with the racket." Joe, Jr. was ten years older than Bobby, but he enjoyed teaching his younger brother how to play tennis.

After Bobby learned the right way to grip his racket, Joe taught him to drive and serve, volley and lob, and gradually Bobby became a good tennis player. Joe persuaded him to enter a tennis tournament, and Bobby won his first match.

15

His second-round opponent was an older, more experienced player, and Bobby didn't have a chance. The other boy ran him from side to side, passed him at the net, lobbed over his head, and practically blasted him off the court. Bobby became angrier and angrier at both himself and his opponent, and when the match was over he threw his racket at the net and stomped off the court.

Joe was waiting for him. "Tennis is a game, Bobby," he said, "not a war. Your racket is definitely not a rifle, and the balls aren't bullets."

"I wanted to win!" Bobby cried, remembering his father's advice.

"You can't always win," Joe pointed out. "But you can always be a good sport. Don't ever forget that."

Thinking over what his brother had

said, Bobby was ashamed of himself, and he promised Joe that he would not lose his temper on the tennis court again. Because Mr. Kennedy was so often away from home on business, Joe, Jr. was almost a father to his younger brothers and sisters.

Joseph Kennedy, Sr. was interested in politics and contributed generously to Franklin D. Roosevelt's presidential campaign funds in 1932 and 1936. When Bobby was twelve, President Roosevelt rewarded his father by making him Ambassador to Great Britain, and the Kennedys moved to London.

Bobby went to an English school, and during his vacations he traveled in many European countries, developing a keen interest in international affairs. While his father was Ambassador, Bobby met many

18

The Ambassador's family visits the Pope at the Vatican. Bobby is third from the left.

of the most important people in the world—people whose very words and acts created international affairs. He met Winston Churchill and Pope Pius XII. One night he stood in the doorway of the American Embassy and greeted the King and Queen of England, who had come to have dinner with the Kennedys.

The next day people all over the world read newspaper reports about the dinner— they even read that Bobby wore a navy blue suit. The Kennedy children were now so well known that sometimes other children asked for their autographs. Ambassador Kennedy was determined, however, that his children were going to become worthwhile members of society.

"Through no virtue of your own," he told Bobby, "you were fortunate enough to be born in the United States under the most comfortable conditions. Therefore you have responsibilities to others who are less well-off."

"What responsibilities?" Bobby asked.

"There are poor people who need help," his father said. "Perhaps you can help them. There are wrongs that need righting. Perhaps you can right them."

Mr. Kennedy's words made a great impression on Bobby. He made up his mind that when he was a man he would try to put his father's words into action.

While the Kennedys were in London it became clear that Adolph Hitler was determined to conquer all of Europe. In September, 1939, Germany invaded Poland, and England and France declared war upon Germany. Bobby's father knew that Germany would most likely bomb England, so he arranged for his family to return to America.

Bobby was sent to Portsmouth Priory, an excellent Catholic boarding school in Rhode Island. Later he transferred to Milton Academy in Massachusetts, to prepare for Harvard. Although he worked hard at his studies, he was never an outstanding student.

Young Bobby becomes a naval cadet (below) following in the footsteps of his brothers, Jack and Joe, Jr., at left.

The United States was now in World War II, and Bobby was anxious to finish school so that he could join the navy as his older brothers had done. Joe, Jr, had become a U.S. Navy flier stationed in England, and Jack was commander of a PT boat in the South Pacific.

After Bobby graduated from Milton, he joined the Navy and was sent to an officer training school in Cambridge, Massachusetts. On weekends he often went to Hyannis Port where his family now lived most of the time, since his father was no longer an ambassador. One day while Bobby was there, two priests came to the house and asked to speak to his father in private.

A few minutes later Mr. Kennedy rejoined his family. His face was pale and sad. "Joe is dead," he said. "His plane exploded while on a secret mission."

Joe's death was a terrible blow to Bobby. He remembered how his oldest brother had taught him to ski, sail, and play tennis. Now he would never see his brother again.

The next year, when a destroyer named the U.S.S. *Joseph P. Kennedy, Jr.* was launched, Bobby and most of his family attended the ceremonies. Bobby's sister Jean smashed a bottle of champagne over the destroyer's bow, and the ship splashed into the water as a navy band played "The Star-Spangled Banner." Although Bobby managed to stand at attention without moving a muscle, there were tears in his eyes.

The war was over before the *Kennedy* was ready to fight, but even so, Bobby wanted to serve on the ship. He left officer training school and volunteered for duty aboard the *Kennedy* as an enlisted man.

On its first cruise the *Joseph P. Kennedy, Jr.* sailed to the Caribbean Sea. Bobby manned a broom, swept down fore and aft, and did other menial chores. Nothing exciting happened during the cruise, much to Bobby's disappointment, but he still gained enormous satisfaction from serving aboard the ship that was a memorial to his brother. Soon after the *Kennedy* returned to the United States, Bobby was discharged from the Navy.

## 3. Football

As soon as he returned to civilian life in the summer of 1946, Bobby pitched in to help his brother Jack win a seat in Congress. Jack was running as a Democrat in Massachusetts, and Bobby was assigned to work in East Cambridge, near Boston. It was a poor district, and Bobby spent many hours climbing rickety stairs, ringing doorbells, shaking hands, and telling the voters that Jack would make a good congressman. It was Bobby's first taste of politics and he enjoyed it. Thanks partly to Bobby's hard work, his brother won the Democratic nomination and was elected in the fall.

That same autumn Bobby enrolled at Harvard College. Although he majored in government, his main interest was in football. Both his older brothers had gone out for football at Harvard, but neither had made the first team or even won a letter. Bobby was determined to do both.

He was less than five feet, ten inches tall, and he was scrawny and underweight. Most of the other players were taller, heavier, faster, and stronger. But what Bobby lacked in size and power he made up in grit and drive. He arrived at football practice an hour earlier than most of the other players, and he stayed there an hour later.

Bobby was kept on the squad, but he did not have a chance to make the first team until his senior year. The opening game that season was with Western Maryland University, and Bobby made the starting line-up at right end. Early in the game he caught a short pass and

raced across the goal line for a touchdown as the Harvard Stadium rang with
cheers.

But Bobby had made his first and last
touchdown for Harvard. At a practice
session a few days later he hurt his leg,
and though he tried to hide the injury

from the coach, he was in such pain that it was impossible.

Bobby's injury ended his dream of making the first team, but he still hoped to win his letter. The last game of the season was against Harvard's big rival, Yale University. If Bobby could play in that game for even a minute or less he would win a crimson H. His leg was much better but it was still taped up, and as the game with Yale began, Bobby sat on the bench with the other substitutes.

The first half ended in a tie, but in the second half Yale outplayed Harvard all the way. Still sitting on the bench, Bobby watched in awe as the Yale fullback, Levi Jackson, a tall, handsome Negro, swept through the Harvard team time and time again.

With one minute left to play, Yale led

by a score of 30 to 21. Bobby knew that there was no hope for a Harvard victory, and he had also given up hope of earning his letter.

"Kennedy!" It was the Harvard coach, pointing his finger at Bobby. "Go in at right end."

Forgetting all about his injured leg, Bobby leaped to his feet and ran out on the field. Harvard kicked off and the Yale receiver made a beeline for Bobby. With the help of some of his teammates, Bobby stopped the runner in his tracks. A few seconds later the final whistle blew. Harvard had lost the game, but Bobby had won his letter.

## 4. Washington

"Run, Ethel, run!" Bobby shouted. Ethel Skakel, racing like a streak of lightning, caught the pass that Bobby tossed and dashed for a touchdown. Blonde, energetic Ethel was visiting the Kennedys at Hyannis Port, and Bobby was teaching her to play touch football. The two had met on a skiing trip in Canada, and since that time they had seen each other often. Like Bobby, Ethel loved sports. She was a champion swimmer, expert horsewoman, and a fine tennis player. Now she was rapidly becoming a star at touch football.

Ethel was the sixth of seven children, and like Bobby, she had determination and spirit. When Bobby enrolled at the University of Virginia Law School, Ethel often came to see him. They fell in love and in 1950, while Bobby was still in law school, they were married.

After obtaining his law degree, Bobby went to work as an investigator for the Department of Justice. When he and Ethel moved to Washington, a new member of the family went with them, their baby daughter, Kathleen, of whom they were very proud.

Bobby liked his government job, but in 1952 he resigned so that he could manage Jack's campaign for the Senate. Jack's Republican opponent in Massachusetts was Senator Henry Cabot Lodge, a much older and more experienced politician, and most

Jack and Ethel listened intently as Bobby
read the first election returns in Jack's
successful race for the Senate.

people thought Jack had no chance to win. Bobby's old determination came forth and he flung himself into the campaign with all the energy he possessed. "Win! Win! WIN!" was now his motto in politics, as it had always been in sports.

Bobby traveled throughout Massachusetts meeting leading Democrats, arranging for Jack to make speeches, and organizing committees to get out the vote. He made many friends and some enemies.

Having had little experience in politics, twenty-six-year-old Bobby Kennedy was quick to express his opinions. He made the mistake of ordering older politicians around. Once when he was talking to the governor of the state, a Democrat running for reelection, Bobby warned him not to do anything that would hurt Jack.

The governor ordered Bobby out of his

office, picked up the phone, and called Bobby's father. "I know you are an important man around here," he said, sputtering with rage. "But I'm telling you this and I mean it. Keep that fresh kid of yours out of sight from here on in."

Bobby was almost too anxious to have his brother elected, and perhaps that was why he was sometimes rude and tactless. Fortunately, he was polite most of the time. He worked harder in Jack's campaign than he had ever worked before. On election day Jack defeated Lodge in a big upset—the only Democrat to win a major office in Massachusetts that year. The campaign enabled Bobby to learn a great deal about politics, and he and Jack proved that together they were an almost unbeatable team.

After the election Bobby returned to

Washington and served as a lawyer on various Congressional committees. After a few years he began his most important work, which was investigating charges of corruption and wrongdoing in labor unions. Bobby was not anti-labor—far from it—but his job was to see that union members were not cheated by their officers.

In the course of his investigations, he discovered that some officers were spending union dues for their own personal enjoyment. Certain union leaders were called to Washington to testify before the committee for which Bobby served as counsel. When one officer was on the stand, Bobby asked, "Did you defraud the union?"

"I respectfully decline to answer," the man said, as was his constitutional right, "because I honestly believe my answer might tend to incriminate me."

"I would agree with you," Bobby snapped. "You haven't got the guts to, have you . . . ?"

Because of this type of incident some of the union leaders thought Bobby was going far beyond the duties of an investigator and was trying to prosecute them. One leader said he was "a young, dim-witted, curly-headed smart aleck," and another called him a "blue-eyed monster."

Many members of the legal profession thought Bobby used unfair methods when investigating the labor leaders, and he began to get a reputation for being ruthless. Bobby, however, believed that these men were wicked and should be punished.

Eventually, some of the corrupt leaders were sent to jail, and as a result many unions made needed reforms. Bobby's work made him a national figure.

# 5. "A Suitcase Full of Votes"

"If Jack can write a book, I can write a book," Bobby said confidently to Ethel after he had been working for the government for several years. Jack's book, *Profiles in Courage*, had recently won the Pulitzer Prize.

"What are you going to write about?" Ethel asked.

"My experiences as a Senate investigator," Bobby answered. So he resigned from his job in 1959 and went to work on his book, which described corruption and crime in America. Called *The Enemy Within*, the book was an immediate success, and it helped make Bobby even better known than before.

His brother Jack was now one of the nation's most promising young men. He had been reelected to the Senate by a majority of almost a million votes. It was the greatest political victory in the history of Massachusetts. Many Democrats were sure that Jack could be elected President of the United States in 1960. Jack and Bobby were enthusiastic about the possibility. Bobby thought that his brother would make a fine president, and he agreed to become Jack's campaign manager once again.

The first step needed for victory was for Jack to win the Democratic nomination. With determination and drive, Bobby traveled all over the country attempting to persuade state delegations to vote for

Jack at the Democratic convention which was to meet in Los Angeles in July. Many leading Democrats promised their support.

The Kennedys were pleased when the Democratic platform committee, which met before the delegates assembled, proposed a strong civil rights plank. It pledged that the Democrats would use federal powers to end all forms of discrimination because of race, creed, or color. Many politicians thought that a candidate for the nomination would lose the votes of Southern delegates if he came out in favor of the civil rights plank. The Kennedys were warned not to take a strong stand in favor of the issue, but they believed that it was morally right to end racial discrimination in America.

When the convention opened, Bobby called a meeting of his campaign staff. Most of them were young men who were there to "sell" John F. Kennedy as the presidential candidate to various state delegations. His eyes red-rimmed from lack of sleep, Bobby climbed up on a chair and announced that he wanted to say a few words about civil rights.

"We have the best civil rights plank the Democratic party has ever had," he began. Bobby went on to say that he and his brother were strongly in favor of the plank and wanted it adopted at the convention. "Those of you who are dealing with Southern delegations—make it absolutely clear how we stand on civil rights," he said.

Although most Southern delegates did vote for other candidates, Jack was

nominated on the first ballot. Senator Lyndon B. Johnson was nominated as Democratic candidate for vice-president.

Bobby was elated by his brother's victory, but he knew that only half of the job was done. Winning the presidential election in November was what really counted. The Republicans nominated Richard M. Nixon, vice-president in the Eisenhower administration, as their candidate for president, and Bobby knew that Jack faced a hard fight.

With Bobby's help, Jack began an energetic campaign, touring states and cities to express his views to the voters.

In the midst of the campaign, the Kennedys were shocked when Dr. Martin Luther King, Jr., the Negro leader known throughout the world for his philosophy of nonviolence, was arrested in Atlanta,

Georgia. He had taken part in a civil rights demonstration and was sentenced to four months at hard labor.

With no thought of the political consequences, Jack telephoned Dr. King's wife to express his sympathy and concern, and promised his help in getting her husband released. When Bobby heard about Jack's call, he felt sure it would lose the votes of many white Southerners. But he was even more sure that what Jack had done was right, and that, in Bobby's eyes, was even more important than winning the election.

As he thought about what he felt was the injustice done to Dr. King, Bobby became so upset that he telephoned the judge who had sentenced him to jail. A short time later the judge freed Dr. King.

When Dr. King's father heard what the

Kennedys had done, he said, "I've got a suitcase full of votes, and I'm going to take them to Mr. Kennedy and dump them in his lap."

On election night the Kennedys and many of their campaign workers were at Hyannis Port. Bobby felt that he had done his work well, and he was confident that his brother would become the next president. But when the returns started to come in, the Kennedys realized that the election would be extremely close.

When the election was still undecided at 4:00 A.M., Jack and all the campaign workers, except Bobby, went to bed. Bobby was too excited and too worried to sleep. He followed the election returns until dawn, and when it was tentatively announced that Jack had squeaked through to victory, he thought, "Maybe it was the

suitcase full of votes that did the trick."

After sleeping for a few hours, Bobby routed the other Kennedys out of bed to celebrate their triumph with a game of touch football. Jack ran for a pass and as the ball sailed just over his head, he leaped into the air, fumbled the ball, and dropped it on the ground.

"That's my brother," Bobby said in mock disgust to the next President of the United States. "All guts and no brains."

## 6. Attorney General

"I would like you to be my attorney general," president-elect Kennedy said to Bobby as they had breakfast together one morning.

"No," Bobby said. "Think of the criticism that would be piled on your head if you gave your brother such an important job."

"I need you," Jack argued. "I need someone I can trust, someone with whom I can talk things over frankly."

"I haven't had enough legal experience," Bobby protested.

"I'm sure you can do the work," Jack said. "And I know that you will never be afraid to express an honest opinion on any subject." Jack finally persuaded his brother to accept the job.

As head of the Department of Justice and chief law officer of the nation, it would be Bobby's duty to protect the rights of all citizens and to see that the laws of the country were obeyed.

Bobby had approved of the Supreme Court decision of 1954 which had ruled that segregation in the public schools and universities of the United States was unconstitutional. When he became attorney general it was his job to enforce this decision.

Soon after Bobby became attorney general, a Negro named James Meredith was refused admission to the University of Mississippi, where there were no black students. Meredith had served his country honorably in the air force and was in every way qualified to attend the university.

In 1962 Meredith obtained a federal court order which demanded that the university admit him. Bobby had carefully followed the case and realized the need for swift action when the governor of Mississippi refused to allow the university to obey the court order.

As attorney general it was Bobby's responsibility to see that Meredith was permitted to enter the university, but first he tried to persuade the governor to change his point of view. Bobby had many telephone conversations with him, but the governor refused to cooperate.

Meanwhile, Meredith was planning another attempt to register at the university.

The young attorney general is interviewed
by newsmen after an important decision.

The governor sent state troopers to bar his entrance, so now Bobby had to act. He ordered two of his assistants to go to Mississippi and set up headquarters at the university. He also sent United States marshals, men appointed to enforce court orders, to protect Meredith and to see that he was not prevented from registering.

The attorney general was at the White House with the President when the marshals escorted Meredith to the campus. The black student planned to register the next morning. Some of the marshals guarded him in a dormitory while others went to their headquarters on the campus.

A large, angry mob gathered at the marshals' headquarters and began to taunt them. They threw eggs, stones, iron pipes, and bottles filled with flaming gasoline at the marshals.

"Two, four, one, three, we hate KENNEDY!" the mob chanted. "Ask us what we say, it's to hell with Bobby K."

As night fell, the mob became even more violent. Bobby, who kept in constant touch with his assistants by telephone, could hear the protestors howling in the background.

"How's it going?" Bobby asked one of his assistants.

"Pretty rough," the man replied. "This place is almost like the Alamo."

"Well, you know what happened to those guys," Bobby said grimly.

A number of marshals were injured, and some of them begged for permission to open fire on the mob. The attorney general refused, but he did let them use tear gas.

It soon became clear that tear gas

The President and his attorney general—
Bobby was both friend and trusted advisor.

was not enough, for the marshals were
fighting for their lives. If they were
overwhelmed, it was possible that the
mob might lynch Meredith.

"There's only one thing to do," Bobby

said to the President. "We must send in soldiers." The President agreed, and thousands of soldiers were rushed to the university. When they arrived the mob at last dispersed. The attorney general had won but at a high cost. Two people were killed during the night and many marshals were hurt.

James Meredith registered at the university the next morning. His courage, together with the support of the attorney general, made it easier for other black students to enroll in previously all-white universities.

Bobby continued to spend a great part of his time and energy helping Negroes. A Mississippi Negro leader, Charles Evers, said, "Mr. Kennedy did more to help us get our rights than all the other attorney generals put together."

## 7. Assistant President

Early one morning in October, 1962, the President called Bobby and asked him to hurry to the White House. The country was facing great trouble.

When the brothers met, Bobby learned that American intelligence officials had found out that Russia was secretly installing missiles and atomic weapons in Cuba, only 90 miles from Florida. "Our security is threatened," the President said. "The missiles will have to be removed."

Bobby agreed, but he hoped they could be removed without resorting to force.

That might start an atomic war which could be the end of mankind.

For the next thirteen days the President held meetings with many of his advisors, including his brother. Some of the advisors wanted to bomb Cuba at once in a surprise attack.

"I'm against that," Bobby argued. "Thousands of innocent civilians would be killed. It would be a surprise attack by a very large nation against a very small one. America's traditions and history will not permit that—there must be another way."

Bobby was in favor of ordering the United States Navy to blockade Cuba. This would prevent Russian ships from bringing missiles and equipment to the island.

While the discussions in the White

House were going on, the missile crisis was making headlines in newspapers throughout the world. Millions of people were afraid that World War III was about to begin.

Finally, the President decided to take Bobby's advice and blockade Cuba. The Attorney General and all those involved in this major decision prayed that the Russians would not attack the United States in retaliation for the blockade.

The Russians did not want war. They sent a message to President Kennedy saying that the missile bases would be removed if the United States would promise not to attack Cuba. Before the President could answer, a more belligerent message arrived from Moscow, demanding that the United States remove some of its bases from Turkey.

President Kennedy and his brother discussed the matter. "Why not ignore the second message and answer the first?" Bobby said.

"All right," said the President. "You write the answer." Bobby and another government official composed a reply to Russia saying that the United States would not attack Cuba if the Russians would remove their bases from the island. The message said nothing about Turkey.

Russia accepted President Kennedy's offer, and the world breathed a sigh of relief.

More and more the President relied on his brother's advice. Many people called Bobby the "assistant President"; he was certainly the second most powerful man in the nation. Bobby was proving to be

Home at Hickory Hill—
everyone joined in the
game of touch football
except the youngest!

an excellent attorney general, and he enjoyed his work tremendously.

He loved his home, too, a spacious, rambling old house in Virginia called Hickory Hill, where he and Ethel lived with their children, who now numbered eight. They had a big swimming pool and whenever he could spare the time, Bobby came home for lunch and went for a swim with his youngsters.

As soon as his car drove up to the house he was always surrounded by his children, who, in warm weather, were usually barefoot and dressed in blue jeans. Bobby conducted swimming races in the pool and taught his children many games. At Hickory Hill he was no longer a public figure but a happy father, proud of his devoted family.

Bobby was also proud of his younger

brother, Ted, who was elected Senator from Massachusetts in 1963. Now all three Kennedy brothers were working in Washington. Their mother now had one son in the White House, one in the Cabinet, and one in the Senate. Someone joked that she ran the most successful employment agency in the world.

On Bobby's 38th birthday Ethel gave a big party for him. President Kennedy and his wife, Jacqueline, could not come because they had to go to Texas the next day. But it was a good party and Ethel, speaking of her life with Bobby, said, "It's all going too perfectly." It was great to be in Washington, great to be a Kennedy, and great to be alive.

Two days after the party, Ethel and Bobby were having lunch beside their pool when the telephone rang. Ethel answered it, turned to Bobby, and said, "It's J. Edgar Hoover." Mr. Hoover was director of the Federal Bureau of Investigation. He had never called Bobby at home before, so this call must be very important.

Bobby picked up the phone, listened for a moment, and then, with an expression of horror on his face, hung up. He turned to Ethel and cried, "Jack's been shot!" Ethel rushed to his side. "Hoover doesn't know how badly Jack's been hurt, but he's afraid it's serious," Bobby said. A few moments later another phone call told Bobby that the President was dead.

Though he was overcome with grief, Bobby could not allow himself to break down. Jack's widow and her two children needed him. He helped his sister-in-law make the funeral arrangements,

Even the children couldn't still the first terrible hurt of the President's death.

and he acted as a father to her children, Caroline, almost six, and John, Jr., whose third birthday was only a few days away.

After President Kennedy's funeral Bobby brooded constantly. He couldn't think of anything except the tragedy. He and President Kennedy had wanted to do so much to make America a better country, but now the chance for the two brothers to work together in achieving this was gone forever.

Ethel tried to cheer Bobby. Though she could not go skiing because she was expecting another baby, she encouraged Bobby to take Jacqueline and her two children on a skiing trip. They went to Colorado and skied high in the Rocky Mountains. Bobby still thought of his brother a great deal of the time, but he was now trying to conquer his sorrow. He remembered how happy Jack had been, and he often remarked that Jack "had led the most wonderful life."

## 8. Senator Kennedy

After Vice-President Lyndon B. Johnson became president, Bobby stayed on as attorney general for a few months. He and Mr. Johnson were outwardly polite to each other, but it was no secret that they were not close friends. President Johnson had his own advisors, and Bobby was no longer the "assistant President."

In the back of Bobby's mind, however, was the thought that someday he himself might become president. He decided to resign as attorney general and run for the Senate from New York. He felt that if he could be elected from such a heavily populated state it would be a step toward the White House.

On his last day as attorney general, Bobby made a speech to his staff. "I like to think," he said, "that our role has been the one suggested in an old Greek saying, 'to tame the savageness of man and make gentle the life of the world.'"

Bobby went to New York and easily won the Democratic nomination for Senator. He started campaigning immediately against Senator Kenneth B. Keating, the Republican nominee. In the midst of the campaign, he was delighted to hear that Dr. Martin Luther King, Jr. had won the Nobel Peace Prize for "the

furtherance of brotherhood among men."
Bobby sent congratulations to Dr. King,
saying that his life and work symbolized
"the struggle of mankind for justice and
equality through nonviolence."

Enormous crowds turned out all over
New York State to hear Bobby speak.
His boyish manner, shy grin, bluntness,
and idealism made him especially popular
with young people. In November the
voters elected him to the Senate by a
large majority.

Hickory Hill was a happy place again,
and Bobby spent as much time as he
could there with his children. He and
Ethel let them have all the pets they
wanted. The young Kennedys had rabbits, horses, ponies, a donkey, a cat,
several dogs, some chickens, roosters, and
ducks. Once the children even had a seal

named Sandy living in the pool. One day Sandy slipped out and flipped his way to the nearest supermarket, creating havoc among the customers. That was the end of Sandy's stay at Hickory Hill.

Bobby had pets too—a large, black Newfoundland dog named Brumus, and Freckles, a cocker spaniel. Bobby liked to take the dogs on walks around Hickory Hill and occasionally on trips in his car.

He couldn't spend as much time with his family and his pets as he would have liked, however, for he was busy in the Senate. With the other New York Senator, Jacob Javits, he sponsored a bill that allowed non-English-speaking Puerto Ricans to vote if they could pass a literacy test in a language other than English. Bobby was pleased when the bill became a law, because it gave full citizenship rights to the hundreds of thousands of Puerto Ricans living in New York.

When Bobby was not working in the Senate, he traveled a great deal and made many speeches. He felt that it was important to keep his name before as many people as possible in the event that he should decide to run for the office of president.

Huge crowds gathered to hear him and his speeches. Bobby often remembered what his father had said long ago about the wrongs that needed righting and the poor people who needed help. He felt sure that it was possible to make the world a better place.

Many of his speeches related to education and children. "Education," he declared, "is the key to the future for every one of our children."

## 9.  Adventure

Early in 1965 Bobby heard that Canada had named a snow-covered mountain in the Yukon for President Kennedy. As a tribute to his older brother, Joe, Bobby had volunteered to serve on the U.S.S. *Joseph P. Kennedy, Jr.* Now, as a tribute to Jack, he decided that he would like to climb the mountain named for him.

Mount Kennedy had never been scaled, but members of the Boston Museum of

Science and the National Geographic Society were planning an expedition to conquer it. When he was invited to join the expedition, Bobby eagerly accepted.

A steep giant of a mountain, 14,000 feet high, Mount Kennedy is near the border between Canada and Alaska. Bobby was not an experienced mountain climber, but he was determined to scale Mt. Kennedy. He flew to the West Coast to join the other members of the expedition, all veteran mountain climbers.

When Bobby telephoned to his family from Seattle, his oldest son said, "Good luck, Daddy. You'll need it."

A helicopter took Bobby to the base camp on the shoulder of the mountain, and early one frosty morning the expedition started for the top. Bobby wore snowshoes, carried an ice-ax, and wore a heavy pack on his shoulders. While crossing the glaciers that ringed the mountain, he and the others were roped together. When they came to a crevasse, a narrow, almost bottomless crack in the ice, Bobby leaped across as if he had been climbing mountains all his life.

He was exhausted when the expedition stopped for the night, and even though a blizzard roared and howled around his tent, Bobby slept soundly. Next morning the temperature was down to zero and the blizzard was still raging, but the men started toward the top.

Soon the sun came out, the wind died down, and Mt. Kennedy towered above the men in all its beauty and grandeur. One steep cliff lay ahead, but when that was scaled, there was an easy slope to the summit. Weary and breathing hard in the thin air,

Bobby inched up the cliff and finally reached
the easy slope.

One of the experienced climbers turned
to him and said, "It's all yours, Senator."
Soon Bobby stood alone on the peak. He
made the sign of the cross and thought of
his brother, for whom the mountain had
been named.

In a few moments another member of the expedition stood beside Bobby. "You did a tremendous job," he said. "Your brother would be proud of you."

Bobby thought of the words written by James Ramsey Ullman, a famous author and mountaineer: "If there's an ocean, we cross it; if there's a disease, we cure it; if there's a wrong, we right it; if there's a record, we break it; and finally, if there's a mountain, we climb it." The words might almost have been written to celebrate that very moment.

A few months later Bobby took Ethel and five of their children on an expedition through the Dinosaur National Monument, a beautiful wilderness area in Colorado and Utah. In prehistoric times dinosaurs roamed the area, and some of their fossilized remains are still there. Bobby laughed when his children were given dinosaur hunting licenses as a joke.

The Kennedys traveled on rubber rafts down the turbulent Yampa River, covering 28 miles on the first day. At night they landed on the riverbank, and Bobby sent the children to gather driftwood for a campfire. Then he took them fishing.

All the older children caught rainbow trout that went right into the frying pan, but seven-year-old Michael had no luck.

"Try again, Michael," Bobby said.

Finally, the little boy landed a huge fish. He was proud of himself until he learned that it was a sucker and not good to eat.

He was about to cry when his father said, "Anybody can catch an old eating fish. But your fish is about as big as a dinosaur. It's a good thing you've got your license."

On the last day of the trip Bobby shot some dangerous rapids in a one-man kayak. As the tiny craft raced down the river, the water boiled and foamed about it. Bobby had never been in a kayak before, but he paddled with all his strength and kept the kayak from piling up on the rocks. Finally, he reached calm water.

Bobby still loved doing dangerous things. Some of his critics claimed he was just after publicity—and he did enjoy being the center of attention, just as he had as a young boy. But more important, he enjoyed testing his strength and courage and keeping in top physical condition. Like his father before him, Bobby encouraged all of his children to become skilled athletes and to enter all sorts of competitions.

## 10.  Bobby Runs for President

Many of Bobby's friends wanted him to run for president in 1968, but Bobby had a hard time deciding what he wanted to do. He believed that President Johnson would run for reelection, and he knew that a president already in office nearly always receives the nomination of his party if he wants it.

From all indications President Johnson wanted it. But many Americans disagreed with the President's conduct of the Vietnam war.

Bobby, who was aware that the President's popularity was beginning to wane, made speeches saying that the bombing of North Vietnam should stop and that peace should be made at the conference table.

It was not long before another opponent of the President's Vietnam policies, Senator Eugene J. McCarthy of Minnesota, decided to try for the Democratic nomination. Bobby watched with interest when Senator McCarthy entered the New Hampshire primary—a special election that gives party members a chance to express their choice for president before the nominating conventions meet.

McCarthy surprised the nation by running almost neck and neck with Johnson in New Hampshire. His excellent showing convinced Bobby that the Democratic party was split and that Johnson could be defeated.

Early in March, 1968, Bobby stood before a large audience, including Ethel and most of his children, gathered in the Senate caucus room in Washington. With the nation watching on television, Bobby said, "I am announcing my candidacy for President of the United States."

He went on to say that the nation must seek new policies "to end the bloodshed in Vietnam and in our cities, policies to close the gap that now exists between black and white, between rich and poor, between young and old."

Some people criticized Bobby for jumping into the presidential race after Senator McCarthy had won in New Hampshire. They thought he should try to help McCarthy become president.

Flanked by Ethel and nine of the children,
Senator Kennedy announces his candidacy
for President of the United States.

Bobby, however, did not believe that McCarthy could possibly win. On the other hand he felt that he, Bobby, had an excellent chance to become the next president. He believed that he would make a good chief executive, and he was excited by the thought of the challenges the next president would have to face.

Now he set out to prove to the politicians who would nominate the Democratic candidate that he could capture votes. He decided to enter as many primaries as he could. The first was in Indiana.

Bobby toured the state, telling the voters that the Vietnam war threatened disaster for the nation, and that the war could be ended if he became president. He also told the voters that he believed he could do much to put an end to the poverty that afflicted so many Americans.

The money spent on the war, he thought, should be used to help the poor.

All over Indiana, Bobby was mobbed by enormous crowds eager to hear him speak. Many people in the crowds were far below the voting age of twenty-one. "I'm going to lower the voting age to seven," he said with a grin.

Shortly before the Indiana primary, Bobby was stunned to learn that President Johnson had decided not to run for reelection. Johnson would not campaign for Bobby, however, because he wanted Vice-President Hubert H. Humphrey to win the Democratic nomination.

Bobby was now more confident than ever that the majority of the American people wanted him to be the next president. He felt sure that he would win the Indiana primary.

84

One night early in April, on his way to address a crowd in Indianapolis, he was shocked to learn that Dr. Martin Luther King, Jr. had been assassinated in Memphis, Tennessee.

Bobby was moved almost to tears when he broke the news to the people who were waiting to hear him speak. He was hunched against the cold and, in the glare of the lights, he looked even smaller than he was. Many people in the audience were Negroes. Bobby begged them not to meet violence with violence.

"Those of you who are black can be filled with bitterness, with hatred, and a desire for revenge," he said. "We can move in that direction as a country. Or we can make an effort, as Dr. King did, to replace violence with compassion and love.

"I had a member of my family killed," he went on, his voice trembling with emotion. "He was killed by a white man. But the vast majority of white people and the vast majority of black people in this country want to live together, want to improve the quality of our life, and want justice for all human beings who abide in our land."

When Bobby finished speaking he telephoned Mrs. Martin Luther King, Jr. in Atlanta and offered to provide a plane to take her to Memphis. Mrs. King gratefully accepted his offer. Bobby and the other candidates stopped campaigning and went to Dr. King's funeral. As the nation mourned, Bobby asked himself, "When will the killing stop? When?"

## 11.  Victory and Death

America was grief-stricken over Dr. King's assassination, but the nation had to go on with the job of electing a president.  Bobby started campaigning again.  He worked harder than ever, and his shoulders slumped with fatigue, but his electric-blue eyes sparkled as he spoke about his dreams for a better world.

Many of those people who came to hear him wanted souvenirs.  They tore buttons from his shirts, grabbed his cuff links, and took his handkerchiefs.  A woman even snatched one of his shoes.

Early in the campaign Bobby's hair was long and shaggy. Some weeks later when he was greeted by a large crowd at an airport, an elderly man held up a big poster that said, "Beautify America—Get a Haircut."

Bobby smiled when he saw the poster, but he had already had his hair cut shorter. "You see what sacrifices I am willing to make to be President," he joked. "I cut my hair."

After easily winning the primaries in Indiana, Washington, D.C., and Nebraska, Bobby started campaigning in Oregon. In one place he was greeted by people waving signs that said, "Protect your right to keep and bear arms." The people with the signs were against gun-control laws, which they knew Bobby favored.

He said that the gun-control laws were

Bobby spent a few quiet moments on the Oregon shore and then returned to the campaign trail and the great crowds that gathered wherever he appeared.

designed "to keep guns from the criminals, the demented, and those too young. With all the violence and murder and killing we've had in the United States, I think you will agree that we must keep firearms from people who have no business with guns or rifles."

Soon afterward the Oregon voters went to the polls and Bobby was defeated. It was the first time he had ever lost an election.

The next important primary was in California, the most populous state in the nation. Bobby knew that he would have to win in California or lose all hope of the Democratic nomination for president. Bobby traveled throughout the state, speaking against the Vietnam war and deploring the fact that so many young Americans were being killed.

"Which of them would have written a symphony?" he asked. "Which of them would have cured cancer? Which of them would have played in the World Series or given us the gift of laughter from the stage? Those young men are our most important national resource. We must bring them back into American life and that is why I run for President of the United States!"

"Sock it to 'em, Bobby!" the crowds roared.

Bobby ended many of his speeches the same way. "Some men see things as they are and say why," he often said, quoting George Bernard Shaw. "I dream things that never were and say, why not?"

On primary day in California, Bobby relaxed at the beach with Ethel and six of their ten children. He and the children swam in the surf. When a giant wave rolled in and two of his children disappeared beneath it, Bobby dived into the wave and brought them back to shore.

That night the Kennedys went to their headquarters in a Los Angeles hotel to watch the election returns on television. By midnight it was clear that Bobby had won the primary.

Bobby went to a large room in the hotel to make a brief speech to his supporters who had gathered there. Standing on a platform, he waved and smiled while the crowd cheered. He thanked the people for helping him win. It was one of the happiest moments of Bobby's life.

He spoke of his friend Roosevelt Grier, the tall Negro who played on the Los Angeles Rams football team and who was standing nearby. "Rosey Grier said he'll take care of anybody who didn't vote for me," Bobby joked.

Then he became serious. He said he believed it was possible to end the divisions and the violence in the United States. "We are a great country, an unselfish country, and a compassionate country," he said.

Victory in California—Senator Kennedy thanks his supporters for a job well done.

A few moments later as he was leaving the room, Bobby himself was a victim of violence. A young man named Sirhan B. Sirhan pointed a gun at Bobby's head and pulled the trigger. Mortally wounded, Bobby fell to the floor.

He was taken to a hospital and while doctors fought to save his life, the nation prayed for his recovery. But he died 25 hours after he was shot.

Many people believe that if Bobby Kennedy had been nominated in 1968 he would have won the election and would have been a great President. But no one can ever know.

Bobby's body was flown to New York City, where his funeral was conducted at St. Patrick's Cathedral. As people all over the United States watched the funeral on television, Bobby's only living brother,

94

Senator Edward M. Kennedy, spoke about him to the nation. In part he said:

> My brother need not be idealized or enlarged in death beyond what he was in life. He should be remembered simply as a good and decent man who saw wrong and tried to right it, saw suffering and tried to heal it, saw war and tried to stop it. Those of us who loved him and who take him to his rest today, pray that what he was to us, and what he wished for others, will some day come to pass for all the world.

After the services Bobby's body was placed on a train and taken to Washington for burial in Arlington National Cemetery.

Thousands of mourners lined the tracks as the train rolled slowly by. Late that night Bobby was buried near his brother Jack, with whom he had dared to dream of a better world for all mankind.

# Date Due

| | | | | |
|---|---|---|---|---|
| FE 28 '7? | AP 7 '74 | AUG 05 '77 | OCT 14 '81 | |
| MY 1 '7? | DE 11 '74 | OCT 24 '77 | DEC 16 '81 | |
| NOV 13 '72 | DE 3 '76 | NOV 08 '77 | DEC 19 '86 | |
| AP 12 '73 | DE 21 '76 | DEC 3 '77 | DEC 20 '86 | |
| 7 '73 | APR 20 '77 | JUL 31 '78 | DEC 21 1988 | |
| NO 7 '73 | MAY 19 '77 | APR 16 '79 | MAY 06 1991 | |
| FE 4 '74 | AUG 05 '77 | APR 23 '79 | NOV 16 1999 | |
| MR 21 '74 | AUG 05 '77 | MAY 8 '79 | | |
| MR 25 '74 | AUG 05 '77 | MAY 16 '80 | | |

PRINTED IN U.S.A.     CAT. NO. 23 231

72054

J
923.2
K

Graves, Charles Parlin
Robert F. Kennedy

OHIO DOMINICAN COLLEGE LIBRARY
COLUMBUS, OHIO 43219